DISCOVER SERIES
PUPPIES

LOS CACHORROS

Pastor Australiano

Australian Shepherd

Basset Hound

Basset Hound

Beagle

Beagle

Bulldog

Bulldog

Chihuahua

Chihuahua

Chow Chow

Chow

Cocker Spaniel

Cocker Spaniel

Dachshund o Perro salchicha

Dachshund

Doberman Pinscher

Doberman Pinscher

Pastor Alemán

German Shepherd

Gran Danes

Great Dane

Pit Bull terrier americano

Pit Bull

Pomerania

Pomeranian

Doguillo

Pug

Rottweiler

Rottweiler

Terrier escoces

Scottie

Shih Tzu

Shih Tzu

Springer Spaniel Ingles

Springer Spaniel

Caniche enano

Toy Poodle

Braco de Weimar

Weimaraner

Labrador Amarillo

Yellow Labradors

Yorkshire Terrier

Yorkshire Terrier

Make Sure to Check Out the Other Discover Series Books from Xist Publishing:

Published in the United States by Xist Publishing
www.xistpublishing.com
PO Box 61593 Irvine, CA 92602

© 2018 by Xist Publishing All rights reserved
Translated by Lenny Sandoval
No portion of this book may be reproduced without express permission of the publisher
All images licensed from Fotolia
First Bilingual Edition

ISBN: 978-1-5324-0770-3   eISBN: 978-1-5324-0771-0

www.ingramcontent.com/pod-product-compliance
Lightning Source LLC
LaVergne TN
LVHW070951070426
835507LV00030B/3488